£ 1.30
net

JAMES POPE-HENNESSY

THE HOUSES OF
PARLIAMENT

WITH TEN PHOTOGRAPHS BY ERIC DE MARÉ

Folio Miniatures

MICHAEL JOSEPH

LONDON

FOLIO MINIATURES

General Editor: John Letts

*Original edition first published in
Great Britain 1945
This edition first published 1975 by
Michael Joseph Limited
52 Bedford Square
London WC1B 3EF
in association with The Folio Press*

ISBN 0 7181 1302 0

PRINTED AND BOUND IN BELGIUM
by Henri Proost & Cie p.v.b.a., Turnhout

PREFACE

James Pope-Hennessy's long essay 'The Houses of Parliament' first appeared in 1945 as the introduction to a photographic record, published by Messrs. Batsford. It remains today the best introduction of all to a curiously undervalued building. Too few take the Palace of Westminster, which was the triumphant result of an awkward and sometimes bitter partnership between architect and designer, as a great work of art. The sheer familiarity of its outline blinds us to its strength and elegance and ingenuity. Many of those who are not familiar with its interior would be overcome by its splendid and glowing colours. It was this aspect of neglect of one of the glories of our architectural heritage which prompted the author, shortly before his death, to agree to a new edition illustrated this time in colour, with photographs specially taken by Eric de Maré. I hope that the final result at last does justice to the brilliance of the interior of a building which certainly has fame enough, but perhaps too seldom for the right reasons.

JOHN LETTS 1974

ACKNOWLEDGEMENTS FOR ILLUSTRATIONS

Nos. 6–15 Eric de Maré
Nos. 1–5 are Crown Copyright,
reproduced with the permission
of the speaker of the House of Commons.
N. 4 John R. Freeman.
Nos. 1, 2, 3, 5 A.C. Cooper.

I

Shaded by plane trees the Albert Embankment lies along the south bank of the River Thames from Westminster Bridge to Lambeth. It runs below the striped stone pavilions of St. Thomas's Hospital and in April (when the plane trees on the embankment are sprayed with buds like yellow beads) gusts of ether from the hospital mingle with the smell of the river water and of the London spring. All down the centre of the Albert Embankment seats set at regular intervals face the parapet of grey Aberdeen granite that overhangs the river. At regular intervals, too, along this parapet the tall bronze dolphins are set. Below each lamp, upon the outer side of the parapet, a great lion's head in granite, a ring in its jaws, stares out across the river. Day after day, ever since they were first put here in the 1860's, these lions have gazed with their dull stone eyeballs at the panorama before them—the new Palace of Westminster, that long and celebrated neo-Gothic structure which contains, as all the world knows, the two Houses of Parliament.

Seen from across the river the Houses of Parliament give a fine illusion of simplicity. Distance eliminates their rich detail and the east front of the Palace (with the great square towers at either end, the central lanterns, the armoury of pinnacles and turrets, crockets and perforated iron-work like spears against the sky; encrusted with ubiquitous armorial achievements; flecked by innumerable niches) looks flat and noble from over the water. At certain hours of the day the London sun, warming into yellow the greyish limestone walls, puts a regiment of vertical shadows between their many windows. At such moments the Palace of Westminster looks in fact as its architect intended that it should look—august.

The earliest guide-books to the new Palace (pink paper-bound pamphlets of the eighteen-fifties, illustrated with thick little wood engravings of ogee arches and royal thrones) emphasised the intricacy and extent of 'this magnificent pile'. They enumerated the rooms (five hundred), the quadrangles (eleven), the separate residences for officials (eighteen). They pointed out the remarkable length of the east front and the beauty of the black and white lozenges

4

on the paving of its terrace. They indicated the amazing height of the clock tower. They directed your eyes now upward to the shield-bearing angels in the parapet bays, now down to the encaustic Minton tiling at your feet. Maybe they intended to bewilder you with their eager descriptions of the hexagonal buttresses, of the oriels and the open arcade work, of the 'chateaux type' roofs, of the effigies of every royalty in English history standing in canopied niches calmly over your head. Subsequent official manuals have gradually toned down these raptures to suit a less robust generation. But neither old nor new guides have succeeded in making a tour of the Houses of Parliament seem either an easy or a straightforward proposition. How indeed could they honestly do so. For apart from all questions of embellishment, the very ground-plan of this highly complicated set of buildings was primarily dictated by the demands of a highly complicated system of government by discussion and debate—the British Constitution. Like this Constitution also the ground-plan of the Houses of Parliament was tempered by tradition. All these lobbies and committee-rooms, libraries, courts and robing-chambers were found necessary to the comfortable working of our version of democratic government. Should some future calamity demolish Barry's iron-framed Palace as completely as the fire of 1834 destroyed the historic buildings that had occupied its site, I doubt whether a smaller set of chambers could conveniently replace it. Might not the very corridors (high, ill-lit and heraldic) be taken as arterial to our liberties?

But though convenience and tradition accounted for the size and position of the new Houses of Parliament, considerations of what was once deemed fitting determined their present form. The old, low, rambling Palace that had crowded for five centuries against the ancient buttresses of Westminster Hall was burned one autumn night in 1834. The committee appointed by King William the Fourth to choose a design for its successor opted for the new, nostalgic style of Gothic Revival architecture. This brave decision aroused a tempest of abuse, and it is even likely that had the fire occurred twenty-five years earlier we might now see a plastered classical senate-house standing serenely beside the Thames. A Grecian Westminster, erected by Nash or Soane under the auspices of the Prince Regent, would now meet the intent constituent's eye as he hurries across Palace Yard to interview his Member of Parliament. A number of factors weighed against a Grecian Westminster, however. One was the incomplete destruction wrought by the fire itself, which spared Westminster Hall and parts of St. Stephen's Chapel. A second was the proximity of the Abbey. A third was the strange conviction then current that Gothic was essentially an English, a national, style. And the fourth was the increasing vogue all over the country for Gothic Revival building. For in the 'thirties 'the long empire of classicism was being broken and the claims of Gothic began to be recognised'. The decision of the Select Committee was the most spectacular public affirmation of these claims to date.

Having decided on the style of the new Palace, the commissioners proceeded by an open competition to determine who should be that style's interpreter. And here we have, I think, the final reason for the peculiar complexity of Westminster Palace. It lies in the lush imagination of its architect, Charles Barry, and in the heavy industry and antiquarian zeal of his assistant, Augustus Welby Pugin. Before considering the Palace any further you must clear your mind of the bewildering enthusiasms of the old guide-books. Ignoring the coat-armour on the elegant painted ceilings, forgetting the spandrels and the brattishing, it is necessary to remember only the explanation of this great and beautiful monument to Victorian artifice. It is the most obvious explanation in the world. The Palace of Westminster was built to fulfil a specific and dignified public purpose. It was designed and erected in a period of unbridled antiquarianism. It was invented, decorated and furnished by two singular Englishmen. Reduced to the three essentials of any other *œuvre*—purpose, date and artist—even the crocketed and labyrinthine New Palace of Westminster seems manageable and unforbidding.

II

Since this essay does not set out to be a history of the successive palaces of Westminster, there is no call to linger over the lay-out of the medieval buildings which together

with their Regency additions were devoured by the great
fire of 1834. In an alcove by a fireplace in the Lower
Waiting Hall stands a small table with a glass showcase
upon it. This case contains a little drab-coloured model of
the old palace. By pressing a electric button you may
illuminate this Gothic doll's house and peer down aerially
into a series of tiny courtyards, on to crenellated towers,
steep chapel roofs and turreted gateways. Once take your
forefinger off the button and the light goes out. Such a
glimpse as this is all that we need take here of old Westminster Palace.

There has of course been a palace at Westminster since
the reign of Edward the Confessor. It has always been a
royal palace and remained until the reign of Henry the
Eighth a royal residence as well. Here the earliest recorded
parliaments (the king and his counsellors) often met. Here
came in 1265 the first shire representatives, summoned by
Simon de Montfort. A century later, when the Commons
had become a distinct and separate assembly, they sat habi-
tually in the Abbey Chapter House, across the water-
meadows from Westminster Hall, while the Lords gathered
in the painted Parliament Chamber at the south end of the
palace. Like other great secular establishments of the Middle
Ages, the royal palace at Westminster contained a religious
brotherhood, the college of St. Stephen, independent both
of the King and of the Abbot of Westminster. The pos-
sessions of this college included the chapels of St. Stephen,
St. Mary, and the small chapel of the pew, together with
St. Stephen's cloisters and some houses for the brethren,
who had the right to pass freely in and out of Westminster
Hall by day. At the Reformation the college and chapels of
St. Stephen passed to the Crown by the Second Chantries
Act of 1547. Edward the Sixth granted the buildings and
gardens of the college to a knight who had fought well on
Musselburgh Field. But while giving Sir Ralph Fane the
crypt chapel of St. Mary he reserved the upper chapel of
St. Stephen which was declared to have already been
'assigned for the House of Parliament, and in which Parliaments were to be held'. And so, by a strange anomaly,
the greatest scenes of English parliamentary history were
enacted during two and a half centuries in a medieval

chapel. But as the decades passed St. Stephen's looked less and less like a chapel and more and more like a debating hall. A false ceiling was installed below the Gothic vault, and in 1706 Sir Christopher Wren panelled the room and concealed the faded frescoes of a saint's legend behind oak wainscotting. It is this converted chapel that we see in the engravings of eighteenth-century sessions of Parliament— the crowded benches, the animated faces under the heavy bag-wigs, the figure of Sir Robert Walpole or of Burke or Fox solemn and gesticulating in the foreground. At the Union with Ireland in 1801 the accommodation in St. Stephen's was found inadequate and some renovation (incidentally leading to the discovery of the old frescoes) took place. The fire of 1834 so ruined the Commons Chamber that it was decided to demolish what remained and build again upon a different site.

The finest feature of old Westminster Palace was undoubtedly the great hall which, with its simple massive walls and angel-laden fourteenth-century roof, survives as one of the most superb Gothic rooms in Europe. Woodcuts, watercolours, or the scale model in its show-case, will give you the outline and appearance of the old palace. To get its atmosphere you have only to enter Westminster Hall. The hall was first erected by William Rufus in the eleventh century, a powerful Norman chamber, the roof supported by two rows of sturdy pillars like those at Durham and pierced by a vent to draw off the smoke from the great fire burning in the centre of the stone floor. These columns were removed under Richard the Second, when the English architect, Henry Yevele, reconstructed the Norman building, Gothicised the blunt windows and collaborated with Herland in the creation of the hall's chief splendour—the carved hammer-beams of the roof. In the reign of George the Fourth Westminster Hall was repaired by Smirke. Later it was saved both from the fire of 1834 and from the depredations planned by Pugin and Barry. As if unable to distinguish between the majestic and the merely ostentatious, the dignified and the ridiculous, Barry was anxious to raise the roof of Westminster Hall to correspond with the proportions of his new palace, and to fill the great empty spaces within it by two avenues of Victorian statuary.

All that in fact he was allowed to do was to move back the great traceried west window, instal a flight of stone stairs at the west end, and make the hall into the main public entrance for St. Stephen's and the two Houses of Parliament.

Since the old Palace had been built as a residence and not as a venue for parliamentary assemblies, the internal arrangements were a little inconvenient. Westwards from St. Stephen's Chapel the Long Gallery led into the Painted Chamber (outside whose windows lay the Cotton Garden and the Thames). Beyond the Painted Chamber was the old House of Lords, the Princes' Chamber, Lords' Committee Room and Black Rod Room. North of the Long Gallery and parallel to it ran the great Court of Requests. The Union with Ireland, which emphasised the practical disadvantages of Westminster Palace as a parliament house, was the occasion of some demolition and rebuilding to the west end of the palace in the early part of the nineteenth century. The architect employed for this work was that benefactor of Londoners, Sir John Soane. Soane was not merely a competent elegant architect and a collector of works of art. He was also a sensible man. The jumble of medieval, renaissance and eighteenth-century buildings which constituted Westminster Palace filled him with apprehension. 'The exterior of these old buildings', he pointed out in his *Designs for Public Buildings*, published in 1828, 'is constructed chiefly with timber covered with plaster. In such an extensive assemblage of combustible materials, should a fire happen, what would become of the Painted Chamber, the House of Commons, and Westminster Hall? Where', he demanded, 'would the progress of the fire be arrested?' Six years later his query received its final answer.

One of the many objections to the old Palace was the great cold which legislators were forced to endure. Complicated systems of heating were installed beneath the flooring of both Lords and Commons. St. Stephen's was heated by an apparatus in the crypt, where pipes, flues and ventilating shafts competed for space with the Speaker's dining-room and the mummified body of a fifteenth-century Bishop of St. David's. A similar system of stove pipes seems to have been in use beneath the wooden floors of the Court of

9

Requests, converted by Smirke at the time of the Union into a temporary House of Lords. It was thus especially incompetent of Mrs. Wright, the deputy housekeeper of the Lords, not to notice, on that Thursday in October 1834, the unusual heat in the Court of Requests. It was afterwards declared that the thermometer of the House of Lords reached, that afternoon, the unprecedented height of sixty degrees. The warmth was even noticed by two gentlemen whom Mrs. Wright was conducting round at half-past four. One of them swore at the official enquiry that the heat in the Lords Chamber was so great he could feel it through his boots, and that the smoke was so thick he could see neither throne nor bar, nor distinguish one square foot of the tapestry on the walls though he stood up against it. It was patent that something had gone wrong. Mrs. Wright, however, thought otherwise and retired to her snug little room. At six o'clock the wife of the doorkeeper, Mullencamp, saw a sinister glitter beneath the doors of the House of Lords. She ran to the negligent housekeeper, screaming: 'Oh, good God, the House of Lords is on fire!' The handful of persons who could be immediately assembled was quite insufficient to stay the course of the flames (which had originated in the careless burning of old talley-sticks in the stoves beneath the Lords' floor). The corridors, lobbies and staircases which had been built and rebuilt, panelled and plastered through the centuries became mere passages for the onrush of the flames. And soon, in the prim, affected language of Brayley and Britton: 'the progress of the fire afforded a *tableau vivant* of not inferior interest'.

The Houses of Parliament on fire! All London turned out to watch the flames turning the old Palace into a great Gothic lantern in the autumn night. In Old Palace Yard three regiments of Guards and part of a troop of Horse Guards strove to hold back the crowds that pressed forward towards the Palace. The fire lit up the towers of Westminster Abbey and shimmered in the windows of Henry the Seventh's Chapel. High in a cloudless sky the bright moon shone, but over Westminster the night air was heavy with a canopy of crimson smoke. So strong was the glare from the fire that passers-by on Blackfriars Bridge could guess its locality precisely, while at Westminster the bridge was thronged, people clambering astride the balustrades and standing on carts down the centre to get a better view. The river, which unhappily was low, was crowded with barges and rowboats, and many thousands of Londoners stood ankle-deep in mud upon the strand for many hours to watch the marvellous sight. So excited were they, so forgetful of the fire's purport and of their city's loss that they greeted each new column of flame by cheering and clapping their hands. The fall of the roof of the Lords' Library, quickly followed by the collapse of its whole façade, aroused particular enthusiasm. At nine o'clock a disappointing lull marred the spectacle when the thick smoke altogether obscured the Palace. But soon fire was seen glittering behind fresh windows, and from the octagon tower and royal entrances the wind unfurled long banners of orange and yellow flame. The Commons committee rooms, Bellamy's dining-rooms and kitchens were now flaming in full view of the crowds upon the bridge. But back in Old Palace Yard a new fear gripped the more responsible of the sightseers. Would Westminster Hall succumb? Not only might the brittle fourteenth-century hammer-beams easily catch alight, but also the wooden scaffolding (for repair work) which was, alas, at present inside the Hall itself. The Prime Minister, Lord Melbourne, took charge of operations to save the Hall. Fire engines were drawn up within it, and water played out of Yevele's windows and up to the hammerbeam roof. Connoisseurs were watching even at this crisis of the fire, and afterwards agreed that the Hall had hardly been so beautifully illumined since George the Fourth's famous coronation feast. At length the coordinated efforts of the firemen, the soldiery and their civilian helpers were successful, and by three in the morning the fire was considered under control. Next day, while city printers ran off broadsheet accounts of the disaster for despatch to the provinces and lithographers hastily prepared coloured panoramas of the burning buildings, officials of the Office of Works drew up a preliminary report on the damage. The damage was very severe. The House of Lords, together with the robing and committee rooms of the Peers, and the Painted Chamber and Royal Gallery had been demolished. The Commons Chamber (St. Stephen's Chapel) had been hopelessly

11

wrecked, and several residences, including that of the Speaker, were quite gone. What had the day before been the proud and ancient Palace of Westminster was now a maze of broken arches, burned beams, rubble, bricks and fallen pilasters, with pools and puddles of water underfoot. Westminster Hall alone stood grand and beautiful amidst the smoking wreckage. At right-angles to it the Chapel of St. Stephen, roofless and windowless, was a delicate Gothic ruin against an autumn sky.

III

The glow from the burning of the Houses of Parliament had not merely been visible all over the metropolis, but out in the evening countryside as well. Travellers on the Brighton coach had seen it before them as they rolled through the Sussex lanes towards London. As they neared the city they learned where and what this fire was. Amongst these travellers on the coach was an architect, a handsome, sturdy man of thirty-nine named Charles Barry. With Manchester and Islington, the city of Brighton had so far been the chief theatre in which Barry had displayed his very great talents; one may even permissibly say his genius. In all these places he had built churches in the new Gothic style. This style, however, he was painfully acquiring (for he was an ambitious man and wished for fashionable employment) against his better judgment and his natural bent. The son of a stationer in Bridge Street, Westminster, reared in the Gothic shadows of the Palace and the Abbey, he had yet learned as a youth in Italy to admire and imitate the villas and palazzos of the Italian Renaissance. In London his only important commissions had so far been an alteration to the Royal College of Surgeons and the building, in 1829, of the Travellers' Club House in Pall Mall. The Travellers' Club, which with the Reform and Bridgewater House, would suffice to remind posterity of Barry's splendid architectural gifts, was criticised at the time of its erection on the grounds that it was a mere copy of the Villa Pandolfini. Poor Barry. An amiable and wordly man, he was pursued throughout his career by angry critics. His Classical buildings were derided as plagiaristic. His Gothic buildings were ridiculed as insufficiently authentic. And his handling of that great

12

public undertaking, the rebuilding of the Palace of Westminster, aroused a tornado of controversy which continued (with pamphlets whirling like autumn leaves upon the wind) for many years after his death. The choice of Barry as architect of the Houses of Parliament raised him at once to the position of chief architect of early Victorian England. It brought him lavish offers from the aristocracy (to rebuild Cliefden and Clumber, Shrublands and Dunrobin; to make a palace for the Earl of Ellesmere in St. James's). It brought him fat commissions from town councils in the provinces. It placed the future of whole areas of London (Westminster, for instance, and Trafalgar Square) in his hands. Yet it also brought him more trouble and rows and frustration than any English architect had endured since Wren had tried to lay out a new city after the Fire of London. It ate up his life and corroded his peace of mind. But as he jumped from the Brighton coach that October evening in 1834, and went and stood all night amongst the stupid wide-eyed crowds in Old Palace Yard, he saw this great disaster (his son and biographer frankly tells us) in terms of opportunity—an unrivalled opportunity for a living architect to achieve immortal fame.

When the first surveys of the damage were completed, and an official enquiry had established the source of the fire, the Select Committee appointed by the King to make recommendations on the rebuilding of the Palace settled to work. The Committee had been appointed in February of 1835 but it was not until the summer that its decisions were announced. There were thirty-four of these decisions. The most significant declared that the new Palace must occupy the same site as the old, and that the style should be 'either Gothic or Elizabethan'. The normal process of open competition was to determine the architect, and entrants were invited to submit plans by the first of November next, a bare five months away. Ninety-seven competitors sent in their designs, many of them drawings projecting buildings only nominally Gothic. Five were chosen from the ninety-seven plans, and from these five Barry's proposals were finally selected. As soon as Barry's triumph had been announced a number of public journals (goaded no doubt by partisans of the disappointed competitors) began to attack

13

him and his design. Soon ill-wishers had arranged an exhibition of the rejected drawings, and Barry's troubles had truly begun. The Commissioners, however, were not to be deflected and by the close of 1837 the coffer dam was started. Three years later the river wall had been completed and Barry's wife laid the first stone of the Palace (at the southeast angle of the Speaker's House) in April, 1840. By the spring of 1847 the House of Lords and its lobbies were ready for use and in 1852 the Commons Chamber was first officially occupied. Meanwhile a second Select Committee had been set up. Its terms of reference, issued in 1841, sounded harmless enough: 'to take into consideration the promotion of the Fine Arts in this country in connection with the rebuilding of the New Houses of Parliament'. This commission, under the presidency of the Prince Consort, and obsessed by the beauties of 'one branch of the Fine Arts, hardly known in this country, viz., Fresco', exasperated Barry. A second source of persistent irritation was the appointment, at much the same date, of Dr. Reid, the inventor of a patent and most impracticable heating system, to superintend the warming of the Palace. Then, too, there was the problem of who should make the clock and bell for the great tower—eventually resolved in favour of a practising barrister who was an eminent amateur horologist, Mr. Edmund Denisor. These and a thousand other difficulties would have been tolerable if Barry had been supported by reliable and sympathetic assistants. But in 1837, even as the first stones of the coffer dam were being lowered into the muddy Thames water, Barry had quarrelled with his chief support—Pugin. The row was not made up until 1844. And in 1852 Pugin, driven mad by the multifarious details of the work and by the exacting demands of his principal, suddenly died.

I do not propose to enter here into an examination of the old controversy upon the authorship of the Palace of Westminster. After the deaths of both Barry and Pugin their sons waged a pamphlet war upon this delicate question, beginning with the famous pamphlet by the younger Pugin aggressively entitled *Who was the Art-Architect of the Houses of Parliament?* Mud was slung in handfuls. The partisans of Pugin accused Barry of taking the credit for Pugin's designs, of underpaying him, of working him to death and of destroying incriminating documents. The Barry faction confined themselves to pointing out that Pugin could not have designed the Palace of Westminster and was merely an employee who finished off and elaborated Barry's drawings and ideas. It is an unsavoury controversy, and one reads the evidence with a steady and impartial dislike for both men growing in one's mind. It is clear that Barry was exacting and a little dishonourable; while Pugin was a quirky fanatic. In such cases it is salutary to turn from the clamour of controversy and listen to the statements of the two men principally concerned. Two clear and definite statements by Pugin are recorded. In one of them he is declared to have said to a friend: 'I could not have made that plan; it was Barry's own; he was good at such work—excellent; but the various requirements conveyed by the plan, which were not of art, and above all the Fine Art Commissioners, would have been too much for me.' A second comment, the implications of which are self-evident, is Pugin's verdict on the whole Palace of Westminster. Passing one day down the river, he pointed to the great limestone building then in process of construction, and turned to his companion, 'All Grecian, sir', he said slowly, 'Tudor details on a classic body.' Spoken by anyone these words are scarcely complimentary. Spoken by Pugin they constitute a severe condemnation of the architecture of the new Palace of Westminster.

For Augustus Welby Pugin was a young man with a mission. His aim was to Gothicise every aspect of Victorian life, starting with places of worship and domestic houses, ending with furniture, ornaments, women's clothes and marriage jewellery. At the time of the Parliament fire he was only twenty-two years old, having been born (in Store Street, Bloomsbury) in the same year as Dickens, Thackeray and Monckton Milnes. His father was French, his mother English; his own character, passionate and industrious, idealistic and excitable, was presumably the outcome of this combination of nationalities. As he grew up he developed a positively precocious interest in Gothic life and Gothic buildings. This interest was closely interlaced with deep religious feelings and in 1834 he became a Roman Catholic. The conversion of a youth who was already well known for his bold admiration for everything medieval, and for the publications in which he urged the adoption of Gothic modes to modern life, was scorned by his contemporaries. Ruskin, who regarded it as a mere aesthetic conversion, declared that Pugin had been 'blown into religion by the whine of an organ-pipe; stitched into a new creed by the gold threads on a priest's petticoats'. This was not strictly true. But all his life Pugin regarded beauty and religion as synonymous, and for him a return to Gothic ways implied a return to the simple religious outlook which he conceived to have been universal during the Ages of Faith. The ugly materialistic society around him could only be fought and changed by a return to Christianity and to Gothic architecture. How strange that this simple, earnest creed should have impelled him to complicate ever more tortuously each building, or fitting or detail which he settled down to design. Single-mindedness produces its own peculiar efflorescence. The results of Pugin's anxiety to convert the Victorians by the strong clear light of the fourteenth century are to be found in such objects as the iron Gothic datemarkers on the library tables at Westminster, or the curious perpendicular umbrella-stands in the lobby of the House of Lords.

In 1835 Pugin did not himself enter for the architectural competition over Westminster Palace. He had made a more attentive study of Gothic than any other living man in England, but several considerations had prevented him from openly sending in designs under his own name. There was his Catholicism, which made the rejection of any drawing of his for the Houses of Parliament virtually certain. There was his modesty of character, which made him feel unequal to the prospect of being sole architect of the new Houses of Parliament. But also there was his extreme, wretched poverty which made it impossible for him to do work for which he was not immediately paid, and for which (should his designs have been rejected) he would never have been paid at all. He did in fact prepare a scheme of his own for the Palace, but this he sold for three hundred guineas to Gillespie Graham, who sent it in as his own. But Pugin made a further four hundred guineas that summer and autumn of 1835. For this sum he sold his knowledge and his talents to Charles Barry, whom he had lately assisted in the detail of a Gothic Grammar School for Birmingham. For five months he slaved day after day (as his diaries show) at drawings for Barry—working drawings, elevations, designs for the groining of the Record Tower entrance, for the King's Stairs, the throne end of the Lords, the lanterns. Barry drew out the plan and sent it to Pugin with the required measurements. But over detail he allowed Pugin considerable latitude. And, even as Pugin's most recent biographer has neatly put it, 'the trouble was that Barry had hired a ghost and had found a collaborator'. In 1837 there was an explosion, and the collaborator refused to collaborate any further. But in 1844 Barry persuaded Pugin to co-operate again, though this time he insisted on being paid by the Government and not by Barry. It made little difference to the pressure of the work, which killed him in the end. Pugin died in 1852, Barry in 1860. A fascinating volume could be written about the building of Westminster Palace—a study in taste, it would be, but also a study in the clash of personalities. The book could reconstruct the origins and course of the various conflicts in which at each stage of the building of the Palace Barry became involved —the conflict with Pugin, firstly the conflict with the Select Committee over money; the conflict with the Fine Arts Commission over fresco; the conflict over the embellishment of Westminster Hall; the size of the royal entrance; the internal arrangements of the Commons Chamber; the heating and ventilation of the whole Palace, and a hundred other subjects. Then, too, there would be the army of sculptors, painters, mosaic-workers, tile-makers, wood-carvers, ironfounders, goldsmiths and silversmiths who were employed to decorate the Palace. But over all of them, and rising above these conflicts, would tower the sturdy figure of Sir Charles Barry. In the Lower Waiting Hall of the Palace of Westminster (a lobby used as a passage) Foley's statue of Sir Charles Barry stands beneath a trefoiled window. The inscription in the window relates the vicissitudes of the Palace of Westminster. It ends: 'The new Palace was designed by Sir Charles Barry who died in the year 1860 and whose statue was placed below in the year 1865 by public subscription'. The statue which is white marble shows the architect seated, his legs apart, one foot thrust forward. In his left hand he holds a marble drawing board upon which he gazes with fixed intensity.

IV

Drawn out in black and white the ground plan of Westminster Palace looks at first glance most strangely asymmetrical. Barry, you think, has jammed together a huggermugger of rectangles behind his long, level, fluted river front. Some of these rectangles are large, some small, some of them are courtyards open to the sky, others halls, chambers and corridors solidly roofed. In the north-western corner of the Palace these squares and oblongs swerve away to link with Westminster Hall which stands as it has always stood crooked to the Thames bank. A longer look, however, reveals the architect's purpose. The Palace has a spine and this spine, stretching from the Victoria Tower Gardens in the south to Bridge Street and the clock tower in the north, contains the House of Lords and the House of Commons, together with their respective lobbies and corridors; the Ministers' rooms; the vast Royal Gallery; and the Queen's Robing Room. Along the spine, in fact, are situated the essential rooms, the very vertebrae of Parliament. East and west from the spine short corridors thrust out like little ribs to join this central line of chambers to the great libraries and the dining-rooms along the east front, to Westminster Hall and the committee rooms on the west. The interstices between the ribs from the eleven courtyards of the Palace—the Chancellor's, State Officers', St. Stephen's, Cloister and Star Chamber Courts on the west, the Royal Court, Peers' Court, Commons, Speaker's, Peers' Inner Court and Commons Inner Court upon the east. In the north-eastern corner of the Palace is the Speaker's Residence; in the south-western corner the Royal Entrance beneath the Victoria Tower. To the north-west lies New Palace Yard, Westminster Hall, and the Members' Entrance. In the dead centre of the Palace, Central Hall shows as an octagon on the plan. From Central Hall the Commons Corridor leads northwards to the Commons Lobby and Chamber (rebuilt after the war), the Lords Corridor southwards to the Peers' Lobby and the Lords Chamber. East-

THE HOUSES OF PARLIAMENT

PLAN OF THE PRINCIPAL FLOOR

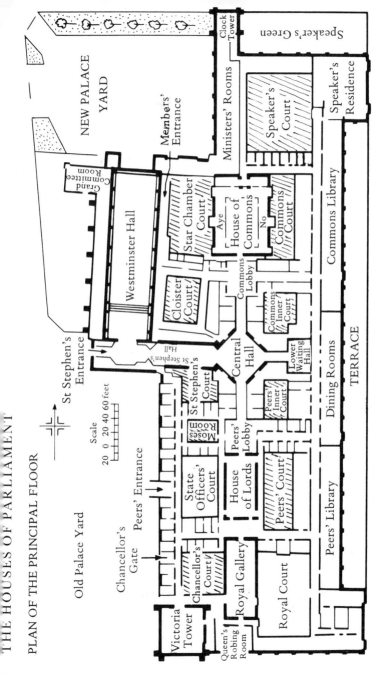

Scale
20 0 20 40 60 feet

Old Palace Yard

St Stephen's Entrance

NEW PALACE YARD

Clock Tower

Speaker's Green

Members' Entrance

Ministers' Rooms

Grand Committee Room

Westminster Hall

Speaker's Court

Speaker's Residence

Star Chamber Court

Aye

House of Commons

No

Commons Court

Cloister Court

Commons Lobby

Commons Inner Court

Commons Library

St Stephen's Hall

Central Hall

Lower Waiting Hall

Dining Rooms

Peers' Inner Court

TERRACE

RIVER THAMES

St Stephen's Court

Moses Room

Peers' Lobby

State Officers' Court

House of Lords

Peers' Court

Peers' Library

Chancellor's Gate

Peers' Entrance

Chancellor's Court

Royal Gallery

Royal Court

Victoria Tower

Queen's Robing Room

ward a corridor and staircase lead down to the Lower Waiting Hall where Barry's marble statue broods. Westwards from Central Hall extends the passageway called St. Stephen's Hall built upon the site of St. Stephen's Chapel and ending in one of Barry's happiest innovations—the stone dais which he added to be southern end of Westminster Hall and which is called St. Stephen's Porch. Standing at the head of the great flight of stone steps which he here inserted, you may survey the length, the breadth, and, above all, the height of this majestic piece of medieval architecture.

'In considering the plan', his biographer tells us, 'Mr. Barry at once saw that Westminster Hall must either ruin any design or form a principal feature in it…. He therefore resolved at once to make Westminster Hall his great public approach, and to carry the public through it and through a hall occupying the site of St. Stephen's Chapel, right into the centre of the site provided.' It was a last valiant effort to give this great deserted building a function in life. Conceived by a Norman monarch to impress his subjects with an appropriate sense of the power and majesty of authority, Westminster Hall was reconstructed under Richard the Second; beauty and elegance were added to the Hall's original grandeur. From the fourteenth century until the opening of the nineteenth, Westminster Hall had two chief uses. It was the recognised and only scene for coronation feasts and for other solemn festivities. It was also the place in which the Courts of Chancery and the King's Bench sat, the southern end of the Hall, beneath the great window, being filled with the docks, desks, benches and canopies of the law. Because of this second function, Westminster Hall became automatically the scene of all the greatest trials in English history—from that of Thomas More to that of Charles the First, from that of Lord Lovat or the Duchess of Kingston to that of Warren Hastings. But also because of the presence of the Law Courts, Westminster Hall became a sort of shopping street. Bookstalls and law-writers' booths jostled each other along the walls, and by the late seventeenth century drapers and riband counters were briskly trading next to these. Barry was wrong when, proposing to raise the height of Westminster Hall and fill it with modern statuary, he urged that it 'should be made the depository... for all the trophies obtained in future wars with foreign nations'. In spite of the banners from Waterloo and from the Peninsula, the theory of war-trophies was no longer in accord with the spirit of the age, nor were the spoils of the battlefield then, any more than now, of consistently decorative value. He was right, however, in his wish to bring the public once more thronging into Westminster Hall as they had done in the old days, swarming about the bookstalls or listening vaguely to the law cases. But with the withdrawal of the Law Courts to the Strand, and the banishment of shops and booths for ever, Westminster Hall was doomed to emptiness, since the English public do not rush to see and hear their representatives debate. Such apathy is evidently a cause for serious reflection or regret, but the inveterate romantic alone will repine over the lost glory and the present lifelessnes of Westminster Hall. This stupendous Chamber, which with the Tower of London has seen more of the chief events and personages of English history than any other building in the country, is now searcely used except for occasions such as the lying-in-state of Sir Winston Churchill. Its floors echo otherwise to the policeman's tramp, the tourist's shuffle or the smarter and more business-like steps of the Member of Parliament in a hurry. Only to those who love to cultivate nostalgia's pallid blooms, only to those with a gleaming talent for evocation, could one recommend a series of visits to Westminster Hall.

From the east side of Westminster Hall an archway with a small staircase once gave access to St. Stephen's Chapel where the House of Commons sat. This archway is now built up, and the way into St. Stephen's Hall (which precisely occupies the site of the Chapel) is from St. Stephen's Porch, where you may pause to survey Westminster Hall. The old Chapel of St. Stephen, built upon a crypt called St. Mary Undercroft, and scene of the Commons debates from the reign of Edward the Sixth to that of William the Fourth, had been burned out by the fire of 1834. Restoration was just possible, but Barry decided against this. If St. Stephen's were reconstructed, he argued, there was a kind of moral compulsion (and this might lead to public pressure) to turn it back to its original holy purpose. And what then could he do, with a consecrated chapel blocking the way between Westminster Hall (his public entrance) and the body of the new Palace? He therefore decided on an ingenious compromise, by which a slightly ecclesiastical perpendicular passageway was built upon the site, while the old crypt of St. Mary Undercroft was faithfully restored to its proper purpose (and later gilded to a positively Byzantine opulence). By this clever arrangement Barry preserved the memory of St. Stephen's, silenced at least some of his critics who declared he was impiously obliterating every trace of the old Houses of Parliament, and gained a lofty and admirable public corridor running from St. Stephen's Porch to Central Hall. This corridor, styled St. Stephen's Hall, is not perhaps the most interesting example of Barry's Gothic manner in the building but it serves its purpose by being graceful, well-lit and fairly spacious. Eight stained glass windows filter the steely London light, and on the ceiling bosses details from St. Stephen's life are carved. English kings and queens from the Conquest to the reign of Henry the Second stand one above the other in their niches at either end. The spaces left above the doors at the east and west ends of the Hall have now been filled by two inspid scenes in mosaic-work, executed shortly after the last war. The panels beneath the windows were also filled at much the same period by a series of story-book frescoes illustrative of English history, painted by Philpot, Sims, Clausen, and their contemporaries. But the most noticeable feature of St. Stephen's Hall is the set of twelve colossal marble statues of seventeenth- and eighteenth-century statesman, which stand on pedestals along the walls. These statues were yet a further source of mortification to Sir Charles Barry. In sketching some of the difficulties with which he had to contend while the Palace was being built, I earlier referred to the Commission set up in 1841 under the chairmanship of Prince Albert to encourage the Fine Arts in the country by employing as many contemporary artists as possible to beautify the new Houses of Parliament. Barry was not asked to become a member of this committee, which settled down to its deliberations without consulting the man chiefly concerned with the embellishment of the new building—its architect. Barry was at once stage examined by the commissioners (who included Lord John Russell, Lord Lansdowne, Hallam and Macaulay), but when the official Report of the Commission was published it became horribly clear to Barry that it was entirely incompatible with his own ideas. The scheme of the commissioners, as Barry's son emphasises, was 'an ideal one, drawn up with great skill and knowledge, so as to cover the whole field of English history'; that of Barry 'was 'a practical one, drawn up with reference to the various halls and galleries of the building and designed to present as grand and perfect a spectacle as possible'. The commissioners' motive, in fact, was literary and historical; the architect's aesthetic and visual. The commissioners won the day, and very soon the chisels and hammers of England's sculptors were at work shaping a series of statues which bore no relation whatever to the scale, style or floor-space of the building which they were destined to decorate. In the same way painters were ordered to work on canvases which had subsequently to be fitted into haphazard positions in the new Palace. The worst offender was Gibson's giant marble group of Queen Victoria flanked by 'Justice' and 'Clemency' which looms in the Princes' Chamber and which even the sycophantic compiler of the 1862 Guide declared 'to detract from the scale of the chamber'. But almost equally intruding seemed the great statesman of Stuart and Georgian days—Selden, Hampden, Walpole, Chatman, Fox, Grattan, Pitt and their companions, gesticulating in the chilly afternoon atmosphere of St. Stephen's Hall. Yet, though they may be out of scale and are certainly out of place, though they lack the vivacious extravagant abandon of real eighteenth-century statuary, these twelve statesmen seem familiar and rather suitable in St. Stephen's Hall. Together with the four brass rosettes which mark the spot on which there stood the Speaker's chair once occupied by Coke or Lenthall, these figures of the great dead serve to recall a great past and remind us of the famous days of English oratory. At the eastern end of St. Stephen's an elaborate doorway at the summit of four steps gives on to Central Hall.

'Except the Lord keep the house their labour is but lost that build it.' This biblical tag, in the Latin of the Vulgate, was baked into encaustic tiling by Mr. Minton and is now trodden underfoot by those who daily mill in Central Hall.

23

Though Barry was on the whole a sanguine man there must have been moments when he felt that his labour was indeed lost or was at any rate incommensurate with his rewards. We have seen that he had to struggle, and struggle unsuccessfully, against the Fine Art Commission; and that this was but one body, one set of authorities out of the many with which he came in conflict. But he had equally to compete with more natural difficulties—the actual terrain, the flow of the Thames, and the lack of symmetry in the original ground-plan of St. Stephen's Chapel and Westminster Hall. Since the river-front was in no way parallel to the east side of the Hall, nor at right-angles to the east end of St. Stephen's and since both these buildings must be brought into a decent relation to the main axis of the new Palace, Barry had tried to shift the river front. He had set back the embankment at one end and advanced it into the river at the other; but this was not sufficiently drastic; there still remained the problem of how to hitch Westminster Hall and St. Stephen's on to the centre of his building without making the whole design ramshackle and top-heavy. His idea was that on entering Central Hall from St. Stephen's you turned right for the Lords, left for the Commons, and continued straight ahead for the river front and the libraries. But how absurd this plan would seem if you entered Central Hall at an angle instead of dead on! The solution he evolved explains the shape of Central Hall: if the room was eight-sided instead of square it would be possible, by judicious adjustments of pilasters and door-jambs, to conceal the slant of St. Stephen's altogether. For this reason Central Hall is an octagon.

It is in this lofty octagon, proportioned like a great parrot-cage, that constituents wait upon a patterned floor to see their Members of Parliament. Barry, whose steadfast urge was to impress (if not to subdue?) the public by the grandeur of their Parliament House, would have liked Central Hall to be considerably higher than it is. Once more he was frustrated—this time by the alleged requirements of Dr. Reid and his bogus heating apparatus which at one moment threatened to take up a third of the cubic content of Westminster Palace. The architect was obliged to content himself with a mere seventy-five feet and a vault studded with two hundred and fifty sculptured bosses. This vault of Central Hall supports the middle lantern tower of the Houses of Parliament and is itself held up by eight sweeping Perpendicular archways which form the eight sides of the octagon. The jambs of these arches are loaded with a further series of statues of English sovereigns beneath jutting, turreted canopies. Four of the arches enclose traceried windows, and the four others stone screens in which carved doors are set. Central Hall is full of telephone kiosks, constituents, policemen, clerks and tourists, and over these loom four white figures of the Victorian age—Russell, Stafford Northcote, Granville and Gladstone, in marble, on pedestals. Yet, despite the massive scale of ornament, and the inevitable detritus of daily use, few will dispute that Barry achieved all the impressive grandeur he sought.

The Commons Chamber, which gave Barry possibly more anxiety than any other portion of the Palace, was first formally occupied by the Lower House in 1852. The authorities had begun by demanding a square chamber, a box in which every Member of Parliament should be brought as close to the Speaker's chair as possible. But it was soon realised that this was both unpractical and contrary to tradition. What was euphemistically called 'the fluctuating nature of the attendance' (which meant simply that less than half the M.P.'s could be counted on to come to the House at the same time) made it seem foolish to have a huge square debating room in which no-one would hear properly. For the over-riding problem, the authorities emphasised, was acoustical. Few members raised their voices when addressing the House. The acoustics of St. Stephen's, with its low false roof and narrow floor-space, heavy galleries, padded seats and three hooped windows of plain glass, had been as good as those of a small country-house chapel. Sonorous and accomplished orators like the elder Pitt could make their voices ring at will down the panelled room and out into the tortuous plastered passage-ways of the old Palace. From 1834 to 1852 the Commons sat in a temporary chamber to which they became so accustomed that they were quite unwilling to abandon its comforts on the completion of the new one. Curiosity was nevertheless acute about the new chamber and a record number of M.P.'s crowded grumbling into it in the first days of the new session of 1852. Their general mood being one of discontent they quickly settled on the question of acoustics by which to vent their ill-will. The ceiling, they decided, was too high. The room itself and the seating arrangements were meagre. The acoustics were ridiculous. It was vain for Charles Barry to plead that his House had not been given a fair trial, that it was being condemned out of hand. He was told he must arrange for the ceiling to be lowered and he could only obey. After this radical alteration, which wrecked the proportions of the room, the architect never willingly entered the Commons Chamber again.

Among the criticisms levelled by contemporaries at Barry's House of Commons was the accusation that he had made it too plain and too 'quiet'. So fashions change that to our eyes his original debating room would probably have seemed over-elaborate and over-full—even when empty of human beings it was too full of wooden panellings and pilasters, of wrought metalwork, buttoned leather stained glass and chiselled stone, too full of intricate Gothic revival shapes and of their yet more complicated shadows. In colour the House was dark. Dark panelling, dark benches upholstered in green leather contrasted with the red seats and the florid gilding in the House of Lords. In the centre at the north end of the chamber stood the Speaker's Chair, a characteristic variation by Pugin upon a traditional theme. Above the Speaker's Chair was the Press Gallery and over that again the Ladies' Gallery. Immediately before the chair stood the great table of the House (a copy of the table designed by Wren for St. Stephen's Hall) with brackets at its lower end for the Mace—that silver-gilt symbol of the Speaker's authority, lent to him by the Crown, and placed upon the table to show that the House is properly constituted, below it when the Speaker leaves his seat and the House goes into committee. The three wigged clerks of the House sat at the table and on the table itself lay the famous despatch boxes (one of them deeply marked by Gladstone's signet ring) which contained the two testaments and a copy of the Members' oath. These boxes, together with all Pugin's careful furnishing, were destroyed by the incendiary bombs of 1941.

Though I do not fancy that Barry himself would have much regretted the destruction of his garbled House of Commons it is in fact a national loss. Aesthetically one may have hesitated about it (though certainly not in agreement with Prosper Mérimée's verdict that the House was an outstanding example of what lack of taste combined with an excess of money could produce); but sentimentally and historically, for considerations of tradition and of affection, we must lament it most emphatically. To the student and to those who care to evoke great incidents of history it is a special loss. Nostalgia does not obey the summons of the will and conjuration of the past demands material assistance from the present. St. Stephen's Hall offers no such aid and so it cannot move us. This chill tiled corridor which Barry built upon the site of the old chapel is too impersonal and we cannot readily recall its associations. Neither the brass rosettes which mark the spot on which stood Lenthall's chair, nor the white marble statesmen under the windows really stimulate the talent for evocation. It is hard to remember that here Elizabeth's Parliament held importunate debates upon her marriage, that here assembled the 'five hundred kings' James feared and those determined men who drew up the Petition of Right and defied King Charles. To the site of this encaustic passage came Cromwell to dismiss the Long Parliament and snatch the bauble, and here spoke Pym and Hampden, Townshend, Chatham and Fox, Canning and the younger Pitt. Barry has made all this seem quite improbable. Yet how charged was the atmosphere of his own Commons Chamber. For in this very room for ninety jears the most fervent verbal contests had been conducted—contests in which idealism strove with ambition, patriotism with self-interest, humanity with the rheumatic forces of reaction. 'From dusk of a summer evening to the dawn of a summer morning', through long winter afternoons or smoky autumn evenings these wooden galleries had been a sounding board for the oratory of the great political leaders of Victorian England.

When the new House began to be used Lord Derby was Prime Minister. Peel had been dead two years and Derby had superseded Peel's successor, Lord John Russell, in February of 1852. By the end of that year he himself gave up the premiership and Aberdeen headed the Government. Early in 1853 Gladstone introduced his first budget, with a sevenpenny income-tax (intended to expire in 1860) as one of its main features. Soon, with the Crimea expedition another and quite disgracefully familiar theme—war expenditure—was for the first time debated within these virgin walls. But disaster at least gives rise to flights of oratory—and it was over the war in the Crimea that John Bright spoke so solemnly of the Angel of Death being abroad in the land—'and I can almost hear the beating of his wings'. But there have been too many famous phrases spoken in the House of Commons in the last ninety years, by too many fine or ignoble characters, too many remarkable events or notorious occurrences to cram into the modest scope of this essay. Lift the lid of the box and how many names fly out. In 1852 there were several Members, and certain outstanding ones, like John Russell and Macaulay, who had first been elected to Parliament in the days before the 1834 fire. It would be neat to find that the move into Barry's new Chamber coincided with a new phase of Parliamentary life, a sort of fresh onrush of personalities or impetus of oratorical power. I doubt if it did. By the early 'sixties the splendid rivalry of Gladstone with Disraeli had settled into its great stride, while the pages of *Hansard* are black with memorable names—Sidney Herbert, Stanley, Cranborne, Villiers, Roebuck, Bright, Lowe, Wood, Milner Gibson, Goschen and dozens more. Towards the end of the century the premiership fell again to members of the Upper House—Lord Salisbury and Lord Rosebery. But the great names continue in the Commons—Randolph Churchill, Joseph Chamberlain, Campbell Bannerman, Balfour, Asquith, Lloyd George; a scale which some may feel descended sharply with the names of Ramsay Macdonald, Baldwin and Neville Chamberlain. How fitting, then, that before the Chamber burned away to ashes in the warm spring of 1941 it had resounded to oratory the equal of any previously pronounced within its walls—the speeches during 1940 of Sir Winston Churchill.

The Commons Lobby, an ante-chamber to the House and in itself a political centre of importance, was badly damaged by the bombs. So too were St. Stephen's Cloisters, built round the Cloister Court by Dr. John Chambers, Dean of St. Stephen's College in the reign of Henry the Eighth and one of Hans Holbein's patrons. Part of these cloisters (with fan-vaulting like bats' wings) had been fitted up to take the overcoats and the hats of Members of Parliament; this part survived, the rest was demolished by the bombing. North of the Commons Chamber, and stretching from it to the Clock Tower, lie the ministerial rooms. Also at the northern end of the Palace are the officials' residences and, north-east along the river front, lies the chain of five superb libraries for the Commons—spacious, civilised, book-scented rooms, book-lined and oak-panelled, with high Gothic windows opening on to the terrace and the broad peaceful Thames. Over the libraries are the committee rooms, each of a different size but all built on the same rather un-interesting utilitarian pattern. These rooms have linen-fold dados, leather chairs stamped with the portcullis, lines of desks and rows of large long tables. The Visitors' Smoking Room is in the same part of the building—that smoking room which was considered a 'luxurious' innovation, de-signed 'with strict relation to its peculiar use' and decorated with a dado of encaustic tiling six feet high.

Opposite the Commons Corridor, on the south side of Central Hall, is the Lords Corridor leading to the Peers' Lobby and the House of Lords.

V

Now that Barry's first Commons Chamber, altered sub-stantially to the whim of a House with more pretensions to self-confidence than culture, has itself been replaced with a more spartan and utilitarian room, it is in the House of Lords, with its attendant Royal Galleries and Robing Rooms and Grand Staircases, that we can best see the genius that emerged from his uneasy partnership with Pugin. For, apart from the breaking of the windows by aerial bom-bardment during the war, and a lengthy period of change of use, when it served to replace the bombed Lower House, this part of the Palace of Westminster remains much as its designers intended it. Moreover, it is a design which both in conception and in detail deserves every inch of its status as a national monument.

For Barry, and for Pugin also, the creation of the Peers' Chamber was an entirely different proposition from their sober task for the Commons. In this aristocratic debating room they knew they could let themselves go, for here none would try to frustrate them, to curb their lavish fancies or bring any element of banality into their conception of a really worthy house for lords. And not a house for lords only. 'The House of Lords', his biographer relates, 'he considered not as a mere place of business, not even a mere House of Lords at all, but as the chamber in which the sovereign, surrounded by the court, summoned to the royal presence the three estates of the realm.' He thought, therefore, that it should partake of royal magnificence, and lavished upon it all the treasures of decoration. The state opening of Parliament, which usually involves a long and ceremonial procession, was in fact very much in Barry's mind. In the Royal Gallery, joining the Princes' Chamber to the Queen's Robing Room, he deliberately designed a sort of processional room through which the sovereign and his attendants might pass. For the frivolous and boisterously irreverent attitude to the Crown prevailing in Regency England had already given way to the new wish to enhance its prestige, and Barry (who was by upbringing and temperament inclined to respect power and birth and wealth) was only too ready to exploit this new enthusiasm. Pugin, less worldly, but his mind aglitter with theories of Gothic kingship, was equally prepared to follow suit, and to make drawings of lozenges and monograms, crowns and sceptres, to put the lily of France beside the English rose upon the ceiling, adding to these simpler emblems the pomegranate of Castile, the portcullis of Beaufort, the rampant lion and all the harts and suns, falcons, dragons and mitres, thistles and harps known to the College of Heralds. The ceiling of the Lords, in fact, was decorated in severest conformity with Barry's favourite maxim—that 'tawdriness' was only produced by 'half-measures' and that if you intended to use gold you should use it thoroughly. Together with the encrusted canopy to the royal throne, this ceiling can be looked upon as the climax or apogee of Augustus Welby Pugin's achievement in the Palace of Westminster.

When completed, the House of Lords won universal

approval. It was really more than the product of Pugin's romanticism blended with Barry's respect for the nobility —it was a microcosm of popular taste in the hungry 'forties. 'Without doubt the finest specimen of Gothic civil architecture in Europe'—the critics were as lavish in their praise as the designers had been in their use of gold. 'Its proportions,' we read, 'arrangements and decorations are perfect. The size and loftiness of the department, its finely proportioned windows, with the gilded and canopied niches between them; the THRONE glowing with gold and colours; the richly-carved panelling which lines the walls, with its gilded and emblazoned cove, and the balcony of brass rising from the canopy; the roof, most elaborately painted; its massy beams and sculptured ornaments, and pendants richly gilded; all unite in forming a scene of royal magnificence as brilliant as it is unequalled.' Similar in general shape to the House of Commons, the Lords was longer, wider and higher, and lighted by eight tall windows in which full-length portraits of English kings and queens shimmered and wobbled in the daylight. Between the tall windows bronze figures of those tough English benefactors, the Magna Charta barons, gaze down on to the tiers of scarlet benches, the Lord Chancellor (in his black and gold robes and white wig, seated on the woolsack), and the throne. At the north end of the room is the bar, of wrought bronze, behind which Speaker and Commons stand when summoned by the sovereign to hear the royal speech at the opening of Parliament. At the opposite end of the room are the dais, with the canopy, the throne and the chairs of state, adorned with the lion and the unicorn, and with bands of crystal eggs. For this is not just one more fanciful Victorian room. It is sumptuous but dignified, showy yet rather grand, full of symbols yet not impersonal. Over the throne, like a dull stain amongst so much gilding, three fading frescoes irrelevantly display scenes in the lives of King Edward the Third, St. Ethelbert and Henry the Fifth as a boy. Like all the gilding and colour of the Houses of Parliament, the walls and ceiling of the Lords are now tarnished by time. But in 1847, when the peers first occupied their new Chamber, a flashing and jewelled prospect shone up to the peeresses and the journalists in their galleries

31

high on the walls. And even the Press Gallery itself was draped, in those early days, with velvet curtains of the purest and richest red.

I fear that I have not done justice to the colour aspect of the Houses of Parliament. The bulk of the exterior of the building is of greyish limestone which can look yellow in some lights: but as the cleaning progresses, Barry's original intention will doubtless reappear more effectively, and the spread of lighter gold will slowly remove the familiar but somewhat sullen aspect, unintentionally conferred on his structure by Victorian grime. Westminster Hall (a place of mortal and sepulchral cold in all weathers) is ice-grey; its roof-beams are the colour of walnuts; the shafts of light that slope through the Gothic windows fill the whole huge hall with a kind of periwinkle or violet glow. For the rest, the various rooms and chambers and passage-ways and lobbies of the Palace are warm brown and dull gold; with scarlet carpets in the corridors (and in the Princes' Chamber and the libraries), and Minton tiles of yellow, blue and russet underfoot elsewhere. The walls of rooms not coated with frescoes or burdened with royal statuary are papered with florid designs of gilt and brown which shimmer dimly in the electric light. The Royal Gallery, a fine wide apartment, tiled throughout its length, contains the two great frescoes by Maclise (*Blücher meeting Wellington* and *The Death of Nelson*). These pictures, forty-five feet long and twelve feet high, have now faded like most of the other frescoes in the Palace and give to the whole Gallery (with its dull gold statues of the English sovereigns on brackets at either end) an autumnal aspect which adds considerably to its beauty. But it is hard to stop writing about this strange, important and very endearing building. Many English buildings, particularly English palaces, create an impression of coldness and formality, even of supercilious hostility, upon the unwary stranger. In contrast with these stands Barry's Palace of Westminster—one of the most amiable buildings in the world.

1. Westminster Hall and New Palace Yard around 1795, by Thomas Sandby

2. A watercolour of Westminster Palace in 1808, by G.F. Robson

3. The fire in 1834 from the same viewpoint: artist unknown

4. *The old interior of The House of Commons in 1710, by Peter Tillemans*

5. *The new interior of the House of Commons in 1858, by Joseph Nash*

6. *St. Stephen's Hall, the West end*

7. *Ceiling and mosaic decoration above the Central Hall*

8. The floor of the Lords Lobby

9. Detail of brass door in the Lords Lobby

10. The Royal Gallery

11. The canopy above the throne in the Lords Chamber

12. The entrance to the Robing Room, Royal Gallery

13. Detail from the fireplace in the Robing Room

14. Door architecture in the Royal Gallery

15. Fireplace in the Robing Room

16. A colour supplement in The Illustrated London News, 1859